Spiritual and Inspirational Thoughts from the Heart

Patricia Ann

MANIFOLD GRACE
Publishing House LLC

Spiritual and Inspirational Thoughts from the Heart
© Copyright 2014, Patricia Ann

All rights reserved. No part of this book may be copied or reproduced in any form without written permission from the publisher.

All scripture quotations are from the King James Reference Bible. © 2000 Zondervan Corporation

Cover design: creativelogoart

ISBN: 978-1-937400-37-8

Printed in the United States of America

Published by Manifold Grace Publishing House, LLC
Southfield, Michigan 48033
www.manifoldgracepublishinghouse.com

Dedication

You can never be prepared for "A Son's Cry" or any cry of a child that holds pain. The dedication of this book goes to the two souls that make my heart rejoice. It is my hope that this book is an outlook on life for my grandchildren, Jadon and Jaila. That it will give them some inspiration and hope as they experience life. Even that experience of "A Mother's Struggle", as she raises her children without the help of their fathers. Even the heartache to inspire one child, who grew up with low self-esteem due to the color of her skin. My "Black Sheep", the one who overcame all her obstacles and became a household fame to some.

Of course, some things in life you have to figure out on your own, like your relationship with God.

Gratitude

As always I would like to thank God for putting so many loving people in my life. Without my loving family, who strengthened me in my time of need, and Gods mercy; who knows where I would have ended up. Thank you mom (Cordalia) for always being in my corner and being that absent parent in my children's life. Thank you to all those who contributed to my well-being while I was growing up.

Not all girls get to grow up having two fathers. I am grateful for both my natural father, Stanley and my stepfather, Edward who raised me.

To my children Blair, Dorothy and Benzel thank you for all the trials and tribulations you took me through; they made me more than a conqueror. My siblings Stanley, Edward, Tonia, thank you for the unbreakable bond that we share and the words of our mother "all that you have is each other" that have kept us close. The love of one being - Jesus, has kept us and spared our lives.

Only God has given the life of His son Jesus so that we may have everlasting life; without even knowing if we are worthy of His blood. In return, all God wants is for us to "Glorify" His name.

Preface

This book was written to help me heal from the heartache and distractions of the past. Writing has helped me to loosen the chains that kept me captive for so many years. Through writing the Lord has put joy back into my heart and taught me how to laugh again. As always, I want to thank God for being there, even when I did not know He was there. More than anything, I want to let others know that no matter when or where, God will never forsake you.

God is only a prayer away and He hears all cries.

Thank You

As a child I was always seen and not heard. The quiet child in the family; that's was who I was. Little did anyone know what was bottled up inside of me. As I grew older, I began to write.

Expressing myself on paper through the mighty works of God, who motivated me. Yes! God, worked on me and brought me out of a hole so dark, that I did not know there was light.

Now, I can be seen and heard.

Table of Contents

Dedication	v
Gratitude	vii
Preface	ix
Thank You	xi
Spiritual Thoughts	1
How Beautiful	2
In Your Time of Need	3
The Tongue	4
Help!	5
No More!	7
I Cried	9
Run and Tell That	11
I'm Not Giving Up	13
Stop Ignoring Me	14
Inspirational Thoughts	15
Set Me Free Lord	16
Who Am I?	17
Out of Something Bad	18
Thou Shall Not	19
The Devil is a Liar	20
Feeding Your Soul	21
Number Rhyming	22
In the Morning	23
Holy Spirit	24
Get it Together	25
Before I Lay Down	26

Contents cont.

Not Anyone	27
Getting High Off Jesus	28
Help Me Lord	29
A Son's Cry	30
A Mother's Struggle	31
Divine Power	33
My Brother	34
Me, Your Mother	35
Keeping it Clean	37
The Holy Ghost	39
Forgiveness	40
Listen	41
In-Between Time	42
Free! So Free	43
Overdose on Jesus	44
Open! The Door!	45
Take it to Jesus	46
Be Still	47
Today	48
Baby Boy	49
Dear Lord	50
Looking	51
I Want to Love	53
I	54
Seek Your Way Out	55
Words of Power	56

Contents cont.

I Stand	57
Have You Ever?	59
Save Our Men	61
Well, I'll Be!	62
Get Me There	63
JESUS	64
NOW!	65
You Got to Know Him for Yourself	66
Negro Women	67
No One to Love Me	69
To My Dearest Son	71
Loved	72
Fallen	73
A Family Prayer	74
EMOTIONLESS	75
Freedom	77
Just Happy	78
Black Sheep	79
Hey Ma	80
Thank You	81
Yeap!	82
Yesterday	83
The Power of Prayer	85
A Voice	87
About the Author	88

Spiritual Thoughts

How Beautiful

The Lord will feed you the desires of your heart.
Talk with God and ask Him questions.
And fear not the answer you await.
For each answer is a stepping stone of reassurance to help you make decisions to become who you are.
During your growing period you will nurture your spirit.
Soon you will realize you are more beautiful inside than you are on the outside.
Eventually, your outside and your inside will blend together and you will glow.

Psalms 139:14
I will praise thee: for I am fearfully and wonderfully made: marvelous are thy works; and that my soul knoweth right well.

IN YOUR TIME OF NEED

MAY THE LOVE OF GOD, COMFORT YOU.

MAY THE BLOOD OF JESUS, BE YOUR SALVATION.

MAY THE PAIN IN YOUR HEART, BE RESTORED WITH JOY.

MAY THE TEARS IN YOUR EYES BE CLEANSING FOR YOUR SOUL.

MAY THE HOLY SPIRIT GIVE YOU PEACE.

MAY THE DIVINE ENERGY, BE YOUR STRENGTH.

MAY YOUR FAITH, BE YOUR GUIDANCE.

MAY YOUR SORROW BE A TESTIMONY FOR THOSE WHO NEED ANSWERS.

MATTHEW 5:4
BLESSED ARE THEY THAT MOURN: FOR THEY SHALL BE COMFORTED.

JAMES 4:10
HUMBLE YOURSELF IN THE SIGHT OF THE LORD, AND HE WILL LIFT YOU UP.

The Tongue

Dangerous are the words that lay upon your tongue.

Vicious is the tongue that captures unrighteous words.

Cruel is the mind that thinketh wicked thoughts.

Wicked is the man who does not obey the laws of the Lord.

Laws of the Ten Commandments which were written in stone.

Stones that carry the blood of Jesus, the son of God.

Blood that is the redemption of our sins.

Sins that were washed away by the crucifixion and the blood of God's son Jesus.

Proverbs 15:26

The thoughts of the wicked are an abomination to the Lord: but the words of the pure are pleasant words.

Help!

I feel so deprived of who I want to be and who I am trying to be.

I feel trapped inside my own mind, held captive, taunting my own thoughts.

I feel blue with the dust of gray weighing over my life.

I feel like I am tired of fighting, tired of going on – tired of being trapped inside my own mind.

I feel like help is far gone and closure in my life is far.

I feel stuck in between walls, trapped under stairs.

I feel like what I need, is nowhere to be found.

I feel distress. I feel like pain is closing in and there is nowhere to run.

Jesus! Where are you? I can't see you. I cannot touch you, where are you?

I feel like praying, begging, pleading, crying, screaming for help.

*And when I did, the door opened,
on the other side was depression!*

Proverbs 12:25
Anxiety in the heart of man causes depression. But a good word makes it glad.

A good word from the book of Psalms when depressed – it reads:

Psalms 46:5
God is in the midst of her; she shall not be moved: God shall help her, just at the break of dawn.

No More

My mind is racing and my soul is fulfilled,
because; now I know what I want.

My smile has changed.

My walk has changed.

My wardrobe has changed,
and my mind has been renewed.

No longer does your smooth talk
lure me, because I know what I want.

No more late night calling man, because
I want an any time man.

No more leave the door open man, because
I want a husband with the key man.

No more ands, ifs, or buts man, because
I want a let's work it out man.

No more where have you been man, because
I want a I'll go with you man.

Spiritual

No more I'll sing you a song man, because
I want a church choir man.

No more winking your eye man, because
I want a mind man, not a lust man.

No more, I'll pay your bills man, because
I want a partner man, a husband man.

No more, shack up man or meantime man,
because I want an all year around seasonal man.

No more, I'll take what you give me man,
because I want a man who knows my desires,
man.

I am grace and grace is me, because
I know what I want.

I am a Winter Woman waiting on a Winter
Man.

Proverbs 18:22
He who finds a wife finds a good thing,
And obtains favor from the Lord.

I Cried

Face down on the floor, one leg twisted, the other bent! "I cried"

Kissing the floor, confused and in shock! How did I get here? "I cried"

Arms stretched out, as if I was running a relay; handing off a baton! "I cried"

"I cried" for all the debt that I could not pay!

"I cried" for all the love I thought was real, that turned out to be only lust!

"I cried" for all the times I reached my hand out and no one reached back!

"I cried" when I thought of all the hardships that suppressed my mind as a failure!

"I cried" for all the times I thought I was moving forward only to be at a standstill!

"I cried" when I thought I had seen the light but, woke to see that I was still in the dark!

"I cried" for my struggle of raising three fatherless children!

"I cried" for all the love and guidance I gave my children who later betrayed me!

"I cried" for all the times I did not allow myself to heal from past wounds!

"I cried" for all the times I was too stubborn and shameful to ask the Lord for help!

"I cried" because despite the casualties of my life I am still here!

Psalm 30:5 – *For his anger endureth but a moment; in his favour is life: weeping may endure for a night, but joy cometh in the morning!*

Run and Tell That

If there is one thing I hate it's people in my business!

So what! If you seen me with my high heels on, and my short shorts!

Who cares! If you seen me with smoke in my mouth, and a cigarette in my hand!

Whatever! You thought you seen me kissing your cousins man!

Damn for-real! It may have looked like me sliding down the pole at the club! But it wasn't!

I'm telling you Mr. Officer! I did not steal anything out of that store; it was that other girl!

Yes! I must admit, it was me who cursed out the mail-lady; after she put my check in my neighbors box.

Girl, bye! They say that for every woman there is three men! And I need all my bills paid!

Please and excuse me! But can you please keep my name out your mouth! You don't know me like that!

Please be patient, God is not done with me yet!

Acts 26: 18 - *To open their eyes, in order to turn them from darkness to light, and from the power of Satan unto God, that they may receive forgiveness of sins, and an inheritance among those who are sanctified by faith in Me.*

I'm Not Giving Up!

I may cry, scream, shout and kick
but I'm not giving up!

My tears, the Lord will wipe.

My screaming shall become words of praise.

My kicking shall become praise dancing.

My shouting shall manifest into deliverance.

Romans 8:18 - *For I consider that the suffering of this present time are not worthy to be compared with the glory which shall be revealed in us.*

Stop Ignoring Me

For the last few weeks I have been feeling the need to get closer to God. Every night I would wake up at the same time 5:30am; and go back to sleep, even though my spirit told me to read my BIBLE. Yes, I refused, rolled over pulling the covers over my head, going back to sleep. Little did I know! Or should I say I didn't want to know, God was trying to prepare me for the next storm. Yes! The storm came and no, I was not prepared. Emotionally shattered in a million pieces, unaware of what to do.

Revelations 3:20 - *Behold, I stand at the door and knock: if any man hear my voice, and open the door, I will come in to him, and will sup with him, and he with me.*

Inspirational Thoughts

Set Me Free Lord

Lord,

I am so tired of this journey

If only I could not look back

My feet drag and my knees weaken

I feel like I am tied to destruction

I need you to show me how to break the chains of hell that keep me bound

How I want to be free, to smile and laugh again!

Lord, set me free

Who Am I?

If only you knew the real me.
Me, the person I really am.
Not the person you want me to be.
To try and change me
is to shatter a fine vase.
For I am alive and full of decisions and choices.
For I am glowing with ambition and striving every day to be better than I was yesterday.
To love me, is to love me for who I am.
I am anointed, tongue speaking and full of the Holy Spirit.
I am your thought when you need a friend.
If you change me, you would not like me.
I am who I am.
For, I am, who I am.
Yes, I have come a long way.
I choose to change into who I am.
I am running water when you need comfort.
I use my eyes to see and my ears to hear and my heart to love.
...So tell me, who are you?

Inspirational

Out of Something Bad

Why did these things have to happen to me?
Why didn't someone hear my cry?
Why didn't someone ask me what's wrong?
Why didn't someone see my tears and feel my pain?
Why do I hurt so bad and cry so long?
Why did it take so long for me to know you Lord?
Why didn't I know I had a spirit?
Why didn't I know God was there all the time?
Why did something bad have to happen to me?
For I am the one who will do the Lord's work.
For I am the one who will hear other children cry.
For I am the one who will console those crying children.
For I am the one who has been made whole.
For I am the Lord's child doing His work.
For I am the one who knows everything is going to be all right.
For I am the one who has turned something bad into something good.
For I am the one who will touch the lives of so many children.
Thank You Lord for your gift.

Thou Shall Not

It's me again; today I had a pretty good day.

I snuck past temptation at the gas station (boy was he handsome).

I refunded my overdrawn check at the bank today.

I also put the pork chops back I stole while shopping at the super market.

I even called my mom and apologized for calling her an old hag.

I pulled the knife out of my neighbors back after she called me a liar.

I also admitted to the police that I was doing ten miles over the speed limit.

And the officer still gave me a ticket for fifteen miles over the speed limit.

Lord, if you just give me a sound mind to sleep through the night, tomorrow will be a better day for me.

P.S. Thank You for your mercy Lord.

THE DEVIL IS A LIAR

SATAN HAS BEEN LYING SINCE THE BEGINNING OF TIME.

IF YOU LISTEN TO HIM, YOU WILL BE MISLED.

FOR SATAN IS NOT WORTHY OF THE TRUTH.

FOR THE SERPENT, SATAN, CANNOT GIVE YOU EVERLASTING LIFE.

IF YOU LISTEN TO THE DEVIL, YOU WILL BE WRONGLY ACCUSED AND YOUR LIFE WILL BE HELL.

SATAN IS KNOWN TO BE IN THE MIDST OF ALL EVIL AND IN THE CENTER OF DESTRUCTION.

SO BE CAREFUL OF WHAT YOU HEAR AND HOW YOU HEAR IT.

AND WHAT YOU SEE AND HOW YOU SEE IT.

TAKE TIME TO ASK THE LORD, IS IT HE THAT IS SPEAKING?

REMEMBER, THERE IS NO LOVE, PEACE, JOY OR MERCY

IN THE NAME OF THE DEVIL.

Feeding Your Soul

They say that reading is knowledge.

To read is to feed your spirit.

When you feed your spirit, wisdom unites inside of you.

With wisdom comes understanding.

With understanding comes a sound mind.

With a sound mind comes leadership.

With leadership comes prosperity.

When you prosper, you have done the Lord's work.

There is always rejoicing when you have done the work of the Lord.

So grab yourself a book of knowledge called the <u>Holy Bible</u> and feed your soul.

Number Rhyming

One and Two; Love and Peace

Three and Four; Joy and Happiness

Five and Six; Singing Harmonies

Seven and Eight; Praising His Name

Nine and Ten; Backsliding and Restoration

Eleven and Twelve; Revival and Bible Study

Thirteen and Fourteen; Cain and Abel

Fifteen and Sixteen; Nondenominational and Baptist

Seventeen and Eighteen; Sinning and Repenting

Nineteen and Twenty; Nuns and Evangelists

In The Morning

Today you will stand tall.

Today you are somebody special.

Today you will say and do the right things in life.

Today you will smile and rejoice.

Today you will have a good day.

Today you are full of pride and dignity.

Today you are more than a conqueror.

Today is your day and you will have a good day.

Holy Spirit

Settled are the skies that watch over me.

Furious are the winds that bind my soul.

Calm are the eyes that protect me.

Peace is the praise that lays within my heart.

Laughter is the glory within my walk.

Jesus is the shadow that leads me.

Silent are the Angels that heal me.

Love is the joy that nurtures me.

Harmony is the music that comforts me.

Get It Together

Yes, it is what you say and how you say it.
You expose your character and take away from your demeanor.
For you are not what you say to others, but now you feel like you are.
Now all those sticks and stones you threw,
you now have to figure out how to pick them up.
Your composure you should maintain.
Your thoughts and attitude should be shared within your spirit.
Never should anyone make you so mad that your pressure rises and your nose bleeds.
You have control and you are in control. You are the one doing the driving.
Sometimes it is better to turn and make a right at the light, down a one-way street.
Take control and smile and your drive will be more peaceful.

Before I Lay Down

Thank you Lord, for accompanying me through the night while I slept. Thank you Lord, for protecting me and my family through the night. Thank you Lord, for creating me to be who you want me to be. Thank you Lord, for giving someone a new outlook on life. Thank you Lord, for healing the sick and feeding the poor. Thank you Lord, for paying my bills this month and next month. Thank you Lord, for giving me patience to deal with your children of all colors.

Not Anyone

Not you or them can tell me how to Love.
Because Love comes from the heart.
Not you, or them can tell me which way to Love.
Because I know how to Love my way.
Not you, or them can tell me how long to Love.
Because Love has no schedule.
Not you, or them can tell me anything about Love.
Because I am the one Loving.
For God has filled my heart with so much Love.

Getting High off Jesus

When I do my dance I'm High

When I shout and stomp my feet

I'm High.

When I sing out of pitch, I'm High.

When I use words like "Thank You",

"You're Welcome", and "Please".

I'm High.

When I speak in tongues I'm High.

When I get High it does not cost

me anything.

So, tell me,

When you get High off Jesus

How do you feel?

Help Me Lord

God, If you could just help me, so that I can help someone else see a way through their fears, doubts, shame, humiliation, sorrow and anger. Lord, work through me so I can work through others to find hope, joy, peace, repentance, love and faith through the mercy of your open arms.

Inspirational

A Son's Cry

My brothers, cousins, nephews, grandfathers and uncles – can you hear me? Stop for a minute and evaluate, not the mother, but the son. Can you see anger and humiliation upon your son's faces? He, the son has only a mother, which has only the strength of a man in her name wo**man**. My brothers, cousins, nephews, grandfathers and uncles who are Kings, STOP! Look upon the faces of your sons.

A hug, a phone call, a lecture, a kind word will make the difference of so many sons crying.

My brothers, find the man who lies deep inside of you and give it to your sons. A son of a brother that will give to another, so many sons will become warriors.

My brothers, Stop! Look! Listen!

Help your sons become warriors of a King as the disciple Paul.

May your sons stand firm at the changing of the stick to a snake.

May your sons have the strength of Sampson, so that they can carry their families through any storm.

And may the wisdoms of the son of God, Jesus, lead him to victory.

My brothers, who are looked upon by so many sons, can you hear me?

Your sons are calling; they are in need of a warrior to lead them.

Can you hear me my brothers? All the support you need is only a prayer away, call on Jesus. Your sons need you, "my brothers."

A Mother's Struggle

After a long restless night of tossing and turning, I was still heart broken.

I woke up with the fragments of last night's argument with my son, heavy on my heart.

The son who knows that there is no one else but mommy to be his provider.

But, I guess when my son had to eat hamburgers for the fifth time this week; it was more than a notion.

Yes! I got mad and pointed in his face and cried tears of anger, and shouted "I am doing the best I can."

Since I'd had a restless night I decided to walk to the grocery store to get what I could with the money I had, hopefully to improve my situation.

As I stood in line to pay for my food, I wondered...

Does anyone see the struggle on my face?
Or see me adding and subtracting with my fingers, hoping not to be embarrassed by not having enough money.

Does anyone see my tears, as the circulation in my hands is cut off, from carrying these heavy grocery bags.

Do I dare stop and rest and feel humiliated, because I look like a bag lady, with groceries in both hands.

My pride would not let me take a ride from a cab driver who said he would not charge me. But, I do not recall any thing in this world being free, "but this struggle".

I have only a few blocks to go Jesus, can you just guide me there; so, that my son can have something different for dinner, during this struggle.

Divine Power

Energy, flows through the pit of my stomach, coiled in a circle and tied in a knot.

Energy, trapped inside the walls of my divine heart.

Energy, waiting to be embarrassed by another soul, to become uncoiled.

Energy, which cannot be seen unless touched by another divine child.

Energy, waiting to burst into comical laughter as loud as thunder.

Energy, of tears of joy being filled with the divine Holy Ghost.

Energy, that I hope to give to another, so they may be divinely inclined.

Energy, I will store away until a storm returns, so that I can smile.

Energy, in the midst of my powerless days and hopeless nights.

Energy, so divinely imbedded in my heart, I savor it to keep me strong until I can be spiritually full again.

Inspirational

My Brother

You have always been one who mysteriously migrates.

You have always been in my heart and in my prayers.

You have always been one who keeps his thoughts bottled up and fights his own battles.

You are the one who is so willing to lend a helping hand and eager to please others.

You never linger around long or want to be a burden to anyone.

You're a big brother to me even though I am the oldest.

You're growing every day and becoming the man you so long to be.

> Prayer has brought me close to you.
> I feel your pain and share your sorrow.
> As your big sister I am here for you,
> whenever you need me. Keep your head up,
> for God is not through with you yet. Big
> brother, you leave an everlasting impression
> on me, your big sister. My impression of you
> is love, ambition, and never giving up.
> "My Brother!"

Me, Your Mother

For nine months I was the shield that protected you.

I fed you from the mouth that I ate from.

I loved you before I had even seen your beauty.

ME, YOUR MOTHER, I carried you in my womb with joy and happiness.

During sixteen years of motherhood I taught you right from wrong and how to be a lady.

But, never would I have thought you would harm ME, YOUR MOTHER.

ME, YOUR MOTHER, would strike not only once but twice.

Now I stand, ME YOUR MOTHER, with fire in my eyes and tears dangling from my chin.

ME, YOUR MOTHER, banged emotionally and physically.

Pain that no one can mend, but God.

Yes, I was dragged through the front streets of hell.

Shattered by dreams of our future, as mother and daughter.

Life's experience has made me strong, and my future looks more graceful, preparing me for the next storm.

Thank God for this story that I may help someone else through the struggle and forgiveness of motherhood. For, our children are not our children, they are children of God. In all due time God will work a miracle and turn those demons within his children - into Angels.

Keeping It Clean

There's an old saying that's been handed down from generation to generation.

The saying goes like this, "Don't try to clean someone else's kitchen if yours is dirty."

This line my mother knew all too well; but from my point of view she didn't know how to clean.

This is black eye number four. And I know the procedures all so well.

First, I wait until the fight is over.

Then I pick up the phone and dial 911.

Next, I go and get my mother a cold towel for her eye, until the police arrive.

They already know us by name, and the police even seem like part of our family.

As usual; he is gone by the time the police arrive.

The police report only takes about ten minutes and I'm in bed by 1:00 a.m.

Now I lay in bed, woke, listening to my mother cry. Crying! My mother screams out, "How could you, after all I have done for you?" I thought "where's my friend."

Inspirational

I lay in bed dazed, looking at the ceiling, asking God to make everything alright once again.

My rapid heartbeat forces me out of bed and down on my knees, so I pray.

> Lord,
> I'm only seven years old and this kitchen thing and keeping it clean is not working. I know my mother was wrong for telling her friends how to clean their kitchen. But Lord, please make my Mother stop listening to her friends when they tell her how to clean our kitchen. Why can't my mother hear you, like I can Lord? Please help my Mama Lord! And I promise I will get up extra early and clean the kitchen.

The Holy Ghost

How I want to dance, to be free.

To express myself through movement.

To leap and reach for the sky with no limitations.

To step into new boundaries with new expectations.

To twist out of old situations and into new dimensions.

To reach into new altitudes leaving behind shame.

To flow into new beliefs and perspectives.

To see my burdens rise up and drift away.

To vision the plan that the Lord has for me.

How I want to dance!

How I want to be free!

Forgiveness

Through forgiveness

the arms of Jesus

will lift you.

And the blood of Jesus

will cleanse you.

The love of Jesus

will change you,

through forgiveness.

LISTEN

Do you hear what I hear?

The birds are singing in harmony
with the bees, and the butterflies
are dancing.

Children are laughing and wiping
tears from each other's eyes, without
being told to do so.

Adults are chanting to the rattle of
thousands of snakes, all in tune.

Horns are blowing near and far as if
someone had just gotten married.

Honey bears are carrying honey to the
celebration led by mountain lions.

Trees bend to the blowing of the wind,
as to kneel in prayer.

The sea is as calm as a newborn sleeping.
Not a worry about tomorrow.

Kangaroos are carrying baskets of fruit to
the people, to be eaten.
"Listen!" can you imagine that?

Inspirational

In-Between Time

I sit and wait until it's my time to shine.

I read, I study, I write and I listen.

I'm waiting on my time to shine,
in between time.

I wait, I pace, I groom.

I stand still, I think, I drive.

While I wait on my time to shine,
in between time.

I help the needy, I pray.

I give words of encouragement to the doubtful.

I give words of wisdom to the sarcastic.

I fret not, those who bash me.

I grow, I mature.

While I wait on my time to shine,
in between time.

I smile with patience, waiting on the Lord to move me. In between time I smile, while I shine.

Free! So, Free

Like a rose petal withering in the wind.
Free at last! Free at last!
Yes! My soul has been saved.
Saved at last! Saved at last!
My soul has been set free,
And the angels are rejoicing.
Saved is what I am!
No one can catch me now, I'm too far gone.
Saved is what I am!
Everlasting life is what I have.
Saved is what I am!
No more chains or wishful thinking.
Saved is what I am!
No time to look back at the past.
Because free is what I am.
My soul has been saved.
I'm Free!
Free! So, Free!

Overdose on Jesus

If you need help in your home, take a dose of Jesus, kneel down and pray.

If you need help on your job, take a dose of Jesus. Write on your memo, "Jesus you are my strength."

If you need help driving to work, take a dose of Jesus. Call on Jesus to protect you from the reckless drivers.

If you need help paying your bills, take a dose of Jesus. Love thy neighbor as you love yourself.

Whatever it is that you need, take a dose of Jesus, He will fix whatever is broken.

Open! The Door!

I have been knocking on your door for years.

You have passed me many times, but never felt my presence.

I have watched you as a child, mature as a young lady.

I have even felt your pain and experienced your joy.

You have never acknowledged me or even recognized me.

I have watched your comings and your goings.

I have stood at your door protecting you day and night.

You have moved now, and I have still been at your door.

I have stood in patience, waiting on you to call me.

You are the only one who is capable of calling me when you need guidance.

You have been walking past doing things on your own, the way you see fit.

Now it is my time to guide you in the right direction. Even though you have never called on me, your life's situations will make you kneel down. And when the time comes the Angels will rejoice because you have opened the door and invited me in. Then you will work for me, spreading my name "Jesus".

Take it to Jesus

If you know like I know, You will take all your pain, frustrations, shame and disappointments to Jesus.

    Pass up the mailman

    your mother

    the bartender

    your brother

    the neighbor

    your sister

    the clerk

    your father

In order to find comfort, direction, healing of a broken heart, you must run to Jesus. No one is more equipped and knows you better than Jesus. The fruit of your lips is your step to healing. Dial Jesus up, on two knees and your response will be better than anyone you would have run to.

Be Still

Stillness is, Now

Stillness is, Listening

Stillness is, Hearing

Stillness is, Discernment

Stillness is, Courage

Stillness is, Surrendering

Stillness is, Closure

Stillness is, Balance

Stillness is, Acceptance

Stillness is accepting the presence of the Lord. Through acceptance you will be able to hear and listen to the Lord. Surrendering to the Lord will help you find closure and courage to be aware of discernment.

Today

Yesterday is a day of the past.

Today is a new day.

Today there is room for improvement, growth and healing.

Today is a new day; give it all you've got, in your soul and in your heart.

Today indulge yourself in the presence of the Lord.

Today is your day; be who you are, rejoice through your divine energy.

Today, work only on today.

Baby Boy

Inside your mother's womb you grow.

Without understanding, you listen to the words from your mother's mouth.

The sound of your mother's heartbeat, soothes your soul.

You sleep, you eat, and you breathe.

Without even knowing the world you will encounter, you stretch your feet, eager to get out.

You listen, you develop, and you wait.

You send signals of heartburn to let your mother know that you still exist.

From a tiny cell to a bundle of joy you were created.

Even though your eyes are not focused on the future, God already has a plan just for you.

So, as you sit and wait, and we anticipate your arrival, you're in the best place to be prepared for life's challenges and accomplishments. Therefore, rest little boy, for God has a plan and many blessings just for you.

Inspirational

Dear Lord

I have heard that it is better to pray for others than it is to pray for yourself. Well, Lord it is my brother, you know him the one that was born after me. If it is ok Lord, I have a favor to ask you regarding his life. Lord I know that you sit up high and look down low; and you see that my brother has not always made the right decisions in life. And Lord, we both know that he has been punished in more ways than just jail. I know that a sin is a sin no matter what sin it is. So Lord, just between you and me; I promise I won't tell if you find favor over your son and my brother. I have heard of your works Lord, of how you made the blind see and the mute talk. Just this once; please save my brother's mind, body, and soul and I promise this will be our secret. But Lord, if you don't find favor over your son, my brother, I'll understand that I have asked this favor too many times. But, my mother said nothing beats a failure but a try. So, Lord I'm trying to do the only thing that I know how to do to save my brother's life and that is run to you.

Love, Your Daughter

Looking

I'm looking for a man who: can get to my heart faster than he can get to my panties.

I'm looking for a man who: is able to stroke my hair before he strokes my breast.

I'm looking for a man who: can carry my worries in his hands and not take advantage of my weak body.

I'm looking for a man who: holds the truth in his heart and holds secrets behind the darkness of his eyes.

I'm looking for a man who: holds me tight while I cry and not wipe the tears that roll down his back.

I'm looking for a man who: is willing to pay a bill and not use my brokenness against me.

I'm looking for a man who: sees my body as a temple and not a cheap thrill.

I'm looking for a man who: detects my pain from afar.

I'm looking for a man who: trusts within himself, to be no more than he really is.

I'm looking for a man who: searches for answers through prayer and not his friends.

I'm looking for a man who: speaks words of encouragement and not words of slander.

I'm looking for a man who: can make love to my mind without caressing my body.

I'm looking for a man who: will invite me to church before inviting me to his bedroom.

I'm looking for a man, but I have yet to find any man to capture my heart.

I Want To Love

I want to smile at the wind; while bending over holding the fat that caresses the side of my hips

I want to laugh so hard at the sight of love; that tears of waterfalls fill my eyes and roll down my cheeks

I want to cry love; while sand emerges between my toes of french manicure of lemon drop scent

I want my heart to flutter at the remembrance of our first kiss; while my stomach fills with butterflies and speckled ladybugs

I want my knees to weaken at the smell of love; while lavender lilies float upon sail boats of toxic oceans

I want to feel rays of energy from lightning that fills the sky while my heart races to yesterday's transmittance of love

I

I would like God to work on me.

To give me looks of wisdom, and a style of characteristics.

To wrap my whole being around love and matrimony.

To give me extravagance over my ordinary life.

To allow grace and mercy to overcome me.

Seek Your Way Out

The miracles of the book of Mark speaks life, restoration of healing, and belief in the Son, Jesus Christ. How He was called on and sought out by those who believed in His mighty works. It speaks of one who just wanted to touch His garment to be near Him but, not visually see Him. Mark speaks of one on her death bed, who was made alive again. Diseases were vanished, just by belief that He is the son of God. Extraordinary miracles that can only be ignited with the gift of God, who looks down low for the next ordinary person to be touched in a way that you have to tell somebody,
"He Lives!"

Words of Power

Hope

Peace   Endurance

Strength

Love   Struggle

Humble

Family   Patience

Joy

Laughter   Fear

Pain

Emotions   Sorrow

Life

Victory   Triumph

I Stand

As I lay in the bed half awake,
I hear the voice
of my oldest child
saying, "what shall we eat?"
my children will be hungry soon

Shall, she take them from their place
of security and love and return them
to a place filled with food
and insecurity

Rambling on about tomorrow and
the day after that, she feels hold no
promises of the contents that lack in
our kitchen cabinets and refrigerator

Even the fact that she, my child
cannot visionally see the outcome
of our predicament, or even the
fact that in her twenty-four
years that God is still with us

A mother familiar to hard times
and suffering as a way of life
but not a lack of love from above

I am believing that all is possible
and, our possibilities are farther than
the human eye can see

Inspirational

Gods mighty works are merciful and
endure to all generations
just keep calling on Jesus
He does hear your humble cry
and we all have our seasons

Have You Ever?

Got down to your last roll of toilet paper
only to have your grandchild, flush it down the toilet?

Seen your last bar of soap melt away in the bathtub?

Not have any gas in your gas tank to get to work and no
money for gas?

Opened your refrigerator only to get only a cool breeze
of baking soda!

Waited on the mailman to only find your check was not in
the mail!

Went to the grocery store, with only five dollars hoping to
make a meal!

Called on a friend, that asked you the same thing you asked
them

Wore the same outfit two days in a row, because you have
no detergent

Caught the bus to an interview, only to get on the bus and it
breaks down

Have you ever borrowed sugar and promised to return it

Have you ever put gas in your car, using only quarters,

Inspirational

nickels and dimes

Have you ever made a list before you prayed

Wished upon an airplane and fell trying to catch a shooting star

Have You Ever.............................?

SAVE OUR MEN

From the time of birth, you were looked down on as a minority

As a child you were deprived of becoming successful, due to your color

In high school you were told, you would not graduate

When you searched for a job, long term; they gave you the graveyard shift

After becoming a proud father, they locked you up for child support

Now you sit in jail, with so many that look like you; not knowing the outcome

Standing before the judge thinking, what do I have to lose; except my hopes and dreams

Free from my own flesh and thoughts, I remember that I have an identity

I am not marked by a number but by the fact that Jesus loves me!

And I will continue not to give up, on myself!

Inspirational

Well, I'll Be!

Today they turned off my lights

then came back and turned off

my phone.

Then I received an eviction notice

from my landlord, who wanted

her last two months' rent.

I shall cry but not commit suicide.

I shall shatter but not be broke.

I shall tremble but not fall.

I shall exhale but not pass out.

I shall laugh and not scream.

I shall drive by, but not shoot.

I shall drink, but not get drunk.

I shall call on the Lord at all times

even though my soul is weak and

my body is fragile!

Thoughts from the Heart

Get Me There

There, is where I need to be.

There, the place where I can lay my burden down.

There, is where the transition from lady to woman takes place.

There, where nothing else matters but, Jesus.

There, is where I am.

There, is where joy, peace, happiness resides.

There, is where love flows throughout your body.

There, the place that I never knew existed.

There, is where I am in the comfort of the Lord.

There, is where I found out who I really am.

There, is where I began to see clearly.

There, is where I need to be, to be reigned on.

There, is where I need to be, to be used by God.

There, is where God gives the blind sight and make the poor, wealthy.

There, is where you learn who the Kings of Kings really is.

JESUS

J IS FOR JOYOUS JESUS.

E IS FOR THE EVERLASTING JOY JESUS GIVES.

S IS FOR SINNING, REPENTING AND REJOICING.

U IS FOR JESUS UNDERSTANDING YOUR CIRCUMSTANCE.

S IS FOR SITUATIONS THAT YOU WILL OVERCOME.

JOYOUS JESUS IS SO UNDER-STANDING, THAT HE FORGIVES US OF OUR SINS SO, THAT WE MAY OVERCOME OUR SITUATIONS AND HAVE EVERLASTING LIFE.

NOW!

Whatever it is that you need to do, just do it!

Don't wait on tomorrow, because tomorrow there will be a new task to conquer.

The time is now!

Do it!

Do it with grace!

Do it as if this was your last battle to get into the heavenly gates of heaven.

Do it in the name of Jesus, and God will have your back.

Now is the time to step out on faith and try Jesus.

Just do it!

Inspirational

You Got To Know Him for Yourself

If you don't know how you're going to make it through your suffering, then you really don't know Jesus.

If you can't see any way out of your sickness, then you really don't know Jesus.

If you don't understand your situation, and you can't see the Glory of it all, then you really don't know Jesus.

If you can't seem to call His name in your time of need, then you really don't know Jesus.

If you can't seem to fight back when Satan has a hold of you, then you really don't know Jesus.

When you know Jesus for yourself, you're able to smile in the midst of a storm. After every storm there is always glory; like at the end of a rainbow. Every storm shall pass. But with Jesus in your life, the storm won't be so long. Your suffering shall not be alone, the comfort of the Lord will lift you. When you know Jesus for yourself, no doctor, no lawyer, no teacher, no friend, can contradict what Jesus has for you.

Negro Women

Fierce as the wind that holds my hair up
I am a Negro Woman

Strong are the muscles that force my lips
to protrude with creases of attitude
I am a Negro Woman

Defined are the cheeks that tell a story of
my ancestors trials and tribulations
I am a Negro Woman

Arched are my shoulders, broad and strong
nine months of being with child, I am a Negro Woman

Curved are the hips that my hands rest upon
I am a Negro Woman

Flamboyant are my breasts that swing at their
own free will, I am a Negro Woman

My eyes, my best kept secret of defense
they keep temptation at bay, I am a Negro Woman

Mysterious are my ears that hear voices of
joy, laughter, accomplishments and disappointments
I am a Negro Woman

Long are the legs that hold my structure, firm
and steadfast as a raging bull, I am a Negro Woman

Toes that curl at every step afflicted with pain
of long labor days, I am a Negro Woman

I am a Negro Woman composed, molded, strong,
free-willed, labored, colored and suppressed

No One to Love Me

Born the only son to my mother, and the third child of my father.

Labeled a statistic by the time I entered third grade.

As a juvenile in middle school, is where my record began.

Given a block number and I.D my high school year.

By graduation, I had my own pictured wrist band and a felony.

Shackled at my ankles and bound at my wrist at age twenty.

A disgrace to those who love me and a joke to those that hate me.

Misunderstood by those who approach me as a gang member.

Inspirational

Tattooed for life with "Death before Dishonor!"

My soul searches and I don't know why, who or what I am!

Lost from the outside in, I am scared just like everyone else.

In search of my hope, my tomorrow, which way do I go?

No male figure to guide me, and no one hears me!

I scream in my dreams, hoping someone will hear my cry!

No one understands, I am just like them!

I need someone to love me, cause I don't love myself.

Don't know how this all began

but I am praying it all ends soon!

To my Dearest Son

To the one I think looks so much like me. I know that your journey has been long, even at the young age that you are. And I know that mentally you can't grasp, the being of your trials and tribulations. I also know that with everything moving around you, you're at a standstill. But, trust me when I say, I am here for you, not against you. I believe in all that you're capable of becoming, not to mention I know your struggles. Even being your mother, I have always been your ride-or-die chick (Lol). And the word on the streets is that you're a Mama's boy! With all that being said, there is someone who loves you too.

One that sits up high and sees the best in you. Someone that can truly work on your behalf. Even though he is the best friend I ever had, I am willing to share and allow him be your ride-or-die. So, today I am letting you go and taking the back seat. Son, I need you to survive and the only way to do this is totally trusting God. I am stepping back and allowing God to have His way. I do realize that I am in the way of what God is trying to do. No longer can I keep you as a little boy! It's time for manhood to be implemented in your life, so I am letting your hand go. But, do not worry, I will be looking and watching your transformation. You can and will be a productive part of society.

Loved

There is nothing wrong with allowing yourself to be loved. Let it go; the past has passed! You can be accepted for the person that you are! Allow yourself to experience the joy and laughter of love.

Fallen

I don't remember at what point in my life, I stopped living.
I don't remember smiling or even caring if I smiled or not.
I knew that I no longer even thought or dreamed anymore.
I knew that outside of my regular routine, there was nothing.
I had convinced myself that there was nothing missing in my life.
I knew that I loved my family dearly, with all my being, but was not sure how I felt about myself.
How did I get here after all the changes I had been through in life.
Scared to admit that I had hit a dead end, in slow motion.
My soul could no longer search, and what would I be searching for?
Within myself I had no answers, and did it really bother me!
Well, in the first place who really cared, if I was standing or had fallen!
At this point thinking was not a thought, nothing went in, and nothing came out. Where do I go from here?
God how I need thee, to bring the sunshine back in my life! We do fall down and God is always there to catch us!

A Family Prayer

Good Morning my Heavenly Father!

As we all wake up this morning in different parts of the world; my siblings Stanley, Edward and Tonia our children and our children's, children.

Our parents and those we are connected to in any form I ask that you be our guide and our shield; that you protect our comings and goings and that you keep us out of harms way; that you allow us to walk in your footsteps today and you cover us with the blood of your son Jesus allowing no weapons formed against us to prosper; that you give us the gift of discernment and fill us with your holy spirit, that you keep us just a little while longer; returning us all home safe and sound in our right mind with the use of all our body limbs. In Jesus name, Amen!

EMOTIONLESS

WHO WOULD HAVE EVER THOUGHT,
THAT YOU HAD NEVER CRIED REAL TEARS
OR
EVEN LAUGHED FROM THE PIT OF YOUR STOMACH UNTIL YOU FELL OVER
OR
EVEN SMILED AT BIRTHDAY WISHES AND CHRISTMAS PRESENTS
OR
EVEN ENJOYED AN ICE CREAM CONE WITH A BEST FRIEND
OR
EVEN PRETENDED TO HAVE A TEA PARTY AND PLAY DRESS UP WITH MOMS MAKE UP
OR
EVEN INITIATE A HUG OR A KISS TO A SIBLING OR A PARENT
OR
EVEN GIVE YOUR CHILDREN THE RIGHT TO LOVE THEIR ABSENT PARENT REGARDLESS
OR
EVEN ADMITTED YOUR WRONG DOINGS AND ASKED FOR FORGIVENESS
OR
EVEN BE A COMFORTER TO THE PEOPLE CLOSE TO YOU
OR

EVEN GOT DOWN ON YOUR KNEES AND PRAYED FOR SOMEONE ELSE
OR
EVEN ASKED GOD TO BREATH LIFE INTO YOU, SO YOU CAN EXPERIENCE WHAT OTHERS ENJOY

Freedom

The right to live in the skin you're in,
without torment or disgrace!

The preference to love who you choose
regardless of ethnics or region!

The right to hold your head up when
you're singled out in a crowd!

The preference to wear your hair afar or
to draw it near your scalp!

The right to acknowledge your struggle
and proclaim your heritage!

The preference to stand for what you believe in.

The right to profess your struggle to the nation.

And a testimony, of you just being you!

Just Happy

I caught myself smiling

and then I started laughing.

I could not believe;

my praying paid off!

Could not believe;

the shift in the atmosphere!

Could not believe;

my spirit was full!

So, I smiled

    and

laughed some more!

God is Good!

Smile!

Black Sheep

They talked about your color, calling you
black and ugly!

They even talked about your dad, having
moved after your birth!

They even bashed your mom, for having
you out of wedlock!

They talked about your gender and
the way you dressed!

They even tried to predict your future,
giving you a jail sentence!

But, what they did not know is that I have
a praying mother and an unconditional God!
They saw in me what you could not imagine!
I am a black sheep in His pasture!

Inspirational

Hey Ma,

Just wanted to write you a few lines to let you know that I feel your pain. I know that a lot goes without saying. That we live each day by faith, hoping, dreaming and even just on a wing and a prayer. Each day we live fighting our own thoughts within us, trying to stay focused and keeping it together. I am always thinking how I can take some of your pain away, besides, the common things we deal with in life, I know it's even harder, when you lose someone dear to you. I know we talk on a regular basis, but sometimes things need to be said and just be obvious. So, just so you know, I love you and if there is anything that I can do to bring joy and laughter into your life I will! Mom, I believe in you and I could not ask for a better role model in my life! Keep smiling and moving forward, because you are my strength, and for those who don't know it, you are One In A Million! I couldn't have made it through my storms without you! Thank you Mom for all you do! I can't imagine living life without you!

Love, your daughter

Thank You,

Jesus

For Always

Leaving

The Door

Open!

Yeap!

I am looking for a few good children!
You do not have to be good looking
or even charming!
But, you do have to be respectful!
Room and food is free if you can
follow directions and clean!
And talking back is not even
manifested in your thoughts!
You have to be able to wash clothes
and come running when I call your
name!
Of course I will take you shopping
to buy your needs - not wants!
But, your pay off will come when you
turn eighteen and get to leave my
house, fully armed to conquer the
world!   Yeap! I'm looking for a few
good children!

Yesterday

Yesterday I was lost, and my mind was distraught. My mind was in conflict with the day and time of the week. As I bathed at the city park at the drinking faucet, I heard a voice. A voice so loud it scared me and I fell. When I rose there was blood dripping from my forehead. While wiping my head with my sleeve, I saw a shadow. A man of many colors stood before me. He smiled as he spread his wings of colors and formed a rainbow. Through this rainbow I could see a pot of gold at the end.

At first I hesitated, I was scared of being sucked into this peculiar being. Then the wind moved me and life came into my body. My heart pounded with joy and my feet leapt with overwhelming rejoice. Suddenly without any recognition to what I was doing; I reached and touched his beautiful wings of rainbow colors. Walking back slowly I could not believe my eyes. My hands were filled with jewels of ruby, diamond, pearls, gold and even silver. Stepping back slowly my heart raced faster and my eyes shined, as if they were black diamonds.

"Should I run?" I asked myself. "If I run the jewels might disappear", I thought to myself. So, slowly I took one step back, not noticing that my appearance had changed. No longer was I wearing rags and my forehead was not bleeding. Not only did I smell good, I was wearing a new suit and new black shoes that matched. I began to rejoice, dancing freely, stumbling on my feet and leaping as if springs were in my shoes. With every tear of joy, I thanked the man of color for his mercy. That was yesterday.

Today, I am just visiting the park where I used to live and call home. The park where I spent so many lonely days hoping, wishing, and begging for food and at night, I prayed. Now my life consists of helping others, like I have been helped. Can you believe it? Today I have my own business. "The House of Color" is what I call my establishment.

Everyone is allowed to enter into my house; it does not matter if you're broke or poor, homeless or not. This house is where you can be heard and only one person can see your pain, hopes and dreams. Never will you be forsaken, doubted or looked down on in "The House of Color". Anyone and everyone who thinks they are nothing should visit this house. No one of any color will feel rejected, because colors all blend together in this house. You can come here to lay your burden down and find yourself. And maybe one day if you let your faith grow, you'll find your rainbow of colors. Faith will lead you to your path of colors. Remember, God is listening to your every mutter.

Yes! I was a nobody, but I also had faith in my only friend, Jesus.

That was "Yesterday."

The Power of Prayer

Today, I saw something that made me smile

something, that made me have a little bit of hope.

It was the still of the morning.

No traffic, but there were birds singing.

There was an elderly lady sitting on the porch.

This old lady had legs crossed, and her hair tied

up like Aunt Jemima as if she just finished cooking

breakfast. But, what really caught my attention,

her head was bowed and her hands were together

(Praying).

I sighed and began to cry!

That was my confirmation, not to give up,

Inspirational

to hold on to the one thing that never changes

THE POWER OF PRAYER!

A Voice

I have always tried to make something good out of my bad situation. Of course, if you're a living soul, you have a story to tell. My story started when I was the age of five. I was raped for a period of years by more than one person. Being terrified of what would happen if I told, I became a child without a voice. It wasn't until I was about the age of sixteen, that I began to write what I could not speak. And tell what my eyes had seen and the pain that I had felt. My heart longed to scream, and my soul boiled to escape fear that overwhelmed me and took away my childhood. For years I walked around searching for me, and who I was. I wanted nothing more than to be the voice of children who were held captive, like myself and could not be heard.

To the little girl who comes to school dirty, never smiles, never interacts and sits in the back of the classroom. I see you and hear you. Whatever it is! Whatever your tender heart is experiencing, you do have a voice! There is nothing greater than the laughter of a child.

In writing this book I started my healing process. That does not mean that I still don't cry or sleep with the light on at night. But what it does mean, is that I am recovering. If you have never seen me, this is your chance to hear me. A voice that is no longer AFRAID!

Thank you Lord, for hearing my cries and never leaving me.

About the Author

Patricia Ann Smith started writing at the age of sixteen, at the age of forty-six she is completing her first published book. She is a single mother of three and a grandmother of two. She is the oldest of her four siblings. Although she was born in Detroit, she left the city as a toddler and grew up being a military brat until high school when her mother and siblings moved back to Detroit. In 1989 Patricia turned her life over to Jesus, making Him the answer to all her worries as a single parent. Even though there is not a lot of educational documentation of what she is really capable of doing, she is truly gifted with writing.

Patricia can be reached via:

Email: Also-AuthorPatriciaAnn@yahoo.com
FB: Patricia Smith